VICTORIAN LIFE

A VICTORIAN SUNDAY

SIMON AND LUCY FAULKNER

Wayland

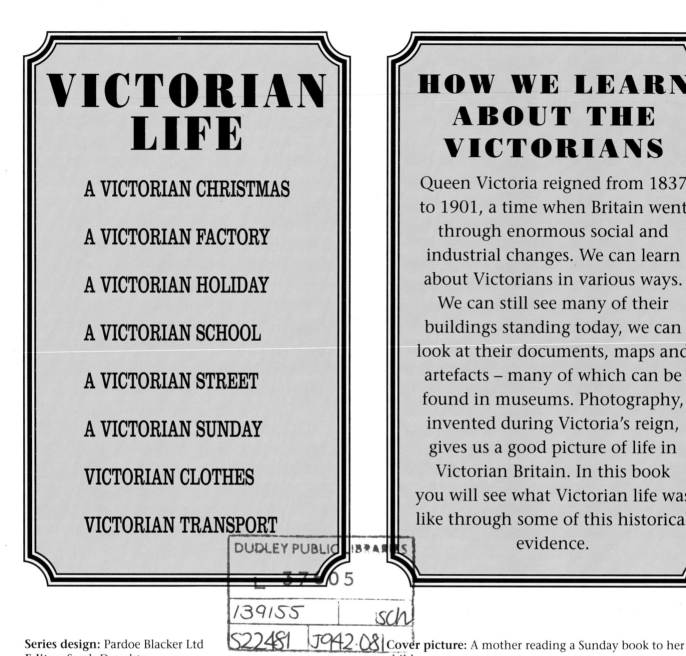

VICTORIAN LIFE

A VICTORIAN CHRISTMAS

A VICTORIAN FACTORY

A VICTORIAN HOLIDAY

A VICTORIAN SCHOOL

A VICTORIAN STREET

A VICTORIAN SUNDAY

VICTORIAN CLOTHES

VICTORIAN TRANSPORT

HOW WE LEARN ABOUT THE VICTORIANS

Queen Victoria reigned from 1837 to 1901, a time when Britain went through enormous social and industrial changes. We can learn about Victorians in various ways. We can still see many of their buildings standing today, we can look at their documents, maps and artefacts – many of which can be found in museums. Photography, invented during Victoria's reign, gives us a good picture of life in Victorian Britain. In this book you will see what Victorian life was like through some of this historical evidence.

Series design: Pardoe Blacker Ltd
Editor: Sarah Doughty

First published in 1993 by Wayland (Publishers) Ltd,
61 Western Road, Hove, East Sussex BN3 1JD, England

© Copyright 1993 Wayland (Publishers) Ltd

British Library Cataloguing in Publication Data
  Faulkner, Simon
  Victorian Sunday. - (Victorian Life Series)
  I. Title II. Faulkner, Lucy III. Series
  941.081

ISBN 0 7502 0691 8

Printed and bound in Great Britain by B.P.C.C
Paulton Books

Cover picture: A mother reading a Sunday book to her children.

Picture acknowledgements
British Library Reproductions 15 (bottom), 26 (top); Mary Evans 22, 24, 26 (bottom); Billie Love Historical Collection *cover*, 5, 6, 10, 11, 12, 14, 18 (both), 20, 21 (bottom), 25, 27; Mansell Collection 7, 17; National Trust Photographic Library 9; Peter Newark's Historical Pictures 8, 16, 19; Victoria and Albert Museum 23 (top); Wayland Picture Library 21 (top); Zefa 13 (bottom). The artwork on pages 7 and 9 is by Annabel Spenceley.

Thanks to Norfolk Museums Service for supplying items from their museums on pages 4, 13 (top), 15 (top), 23 (bottom).

All commissioned photography by GGS Photo Graphics.

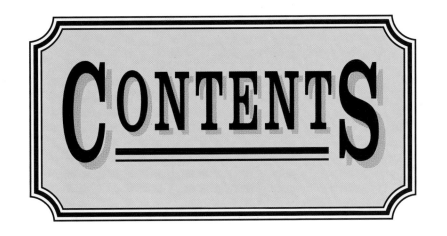

CONTENTS

SUNDAY IS SPECIAL

No jokes, no games, and everyone on their best behaviour: was this the Victorian Sunday? In Victorian Britain, most people were Christians and felt that Sunday should be special, a day of rest given by God. Everyday clothes and activities were not good enough for Sunday. Anybody who forgot this would find themselves frowned upon.

DAY OF REST

Victorians had a strong sense of duty. God had given each person a place in life and tasks to do. Even having a day of rest did not mean doing whatever you felt like. The day was spent in ways which showed respect and gratitude to God. Normal work and play were unsuitable. Shops were shut, although you could buy bread on Sunday morning and milk before 9 am or after 4 pm. Surprisingly, letters were delivered on Sunday.

People were expected to do their 'Sunday duty' and go to church or chapel at least once. Those who worked as servants would go to church but then might have half the day to themselves.

A Victorian calendar.

FAMILY DAY

Sunday was a family day. For many working people, Sunday was their only day off. It was the one day when the whole family could be together.

In rich households there would be a servant called a nurse who looked after the children. For most of the week the children would see very little of their parents. But on a Sunday, dressed in their best clothes and on their best behaviour, children would share the grown-ups' meals and spend time with their parents and the other adults of the family. This photograph shows how three generations of a family would have dressed on a Sunday.

A family at home in 1888.

Do you enjoy wearing your best clothes? Victorian children probably had less choice about their clothes than you do. They were put into clothes thought suitable for their age and sex, almost like a uniform. Nearly every Victorian child had one set of clothes they would keep for Sunday best.

SUNDAY FINERY

Victorian children's best clothes were not very comfortable. They were often easily spoilt. If this boy on the right climbed a tree his white suit would be ruined, and if his sister ran in the garden she might tear a frill. Although they might feel rather grand in their finery, putting on Sunday clothes meant putting on Sunday manners. Sometimes in order to take care of Sunday clothes, children changed up to three times a day, only putting on their best to go out.

Children in early Victorian fashions.

UNDERGARMENTS

A girl in the 1800s wore two pairs of combinations – one made of wool and the other of cotton. Combinations were one-piece garments – made up of a vest and pants which covered down to the knees. A pair of stays was worn on the upper part of the body, a petticoat, and on top of all this, a dress.

Boys wore combinations as undergarments too. Over the combinations they wore shirts and suits. Sailor suits were popular for boys. Both boys and girls wore hats on Sundays.

WASHING

It was important to have best clothes clean, dry and ironed ready for Sunday. Monday was the usual day for washing. If the family was poor and had few clothes, washing had to be done on Sunday. It was the only chance to wash a man's working suit while he wore his best suit. If he did not have one, he stayed in bed!

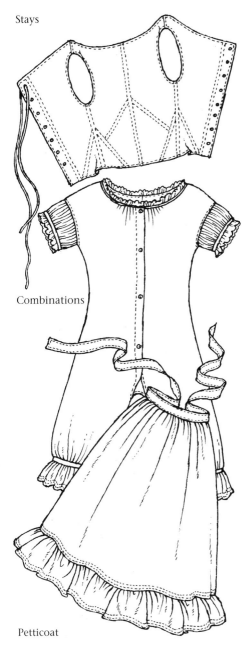

Stays

Combinations

Petticoat

The undergarments worn by Victorian girls.

Sunday morning in a working-class home, London 1875.

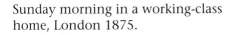

SUNDAY MEALS

If you travelled back in time to a Victorian household, you might be surprised by the food. In a poor family, it would seem very dull, and you might complain that there was not enough to eat. If you were in a rich family, you might be amazed at the amount of food eaten.

Sunday meals were usually bigger and better than weekday meals. The difference was more important for poorer people, whose Sunday meals would bring the only treats they had.

Breakfast, 1888.

BREAKFAST

In a poor family, breakfast was usually bread with jam or lard, and tea. Anything extra, such as an egg, would be for the father on Sunday. In rich families, dinner was late and breakfast could be a large meal with hot dishes of eggs, kidneys, bacon, sausages and chops. Then there might be cold ham, tongue and pies, plus muffins, toast, tea and coffee. Not everybody had the appetite for such a large meal. This family is satisfied with eggs, bread and coffee.

MEAT FOR DINNER

Working people had Sunday dinner in the middle of the day. It might be the only day of the week they had meat, even if it was only small pieces in their 'pudding'. The pudding, like a dumpling, was wrapped in a cloth and boiled in the pot with vegetables. If the family could afford a piece of meat to roast, it could be hung before the fire, or cooked on a spit with a tray to catch the dripping.

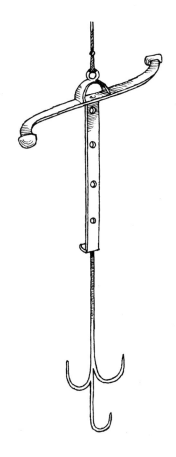

A spit for cooking meat.

KITCHEN RANGE

Better-off families had a kitchen range, similar to the one shown here. A kitchen range would have several ovens which could be used for roasting and baking. When people could afford to, it was normal to eat several dishes for each course. On a kitchen range, several types of meat could be cooked at the same time, so roast meat could be served at the same time as boiled meat.

This is the Sunday dinner that was served in a successful builder's house in Oxfordshire in the 1880s. Relatives came for the day, so there were four adults and four children to eat the meal, and one servant to help with the cooking.

> Roast leg of lamb
> Two boiled fowls, garnished with slices of ham
> Jellies and cheesecakes

AFTERNOON TEA

Many households, rich and poor, had a cake specially baked for Sunday. In poor families this would appear at the last meal of the day, along with bread and butter. For the better off, there would also be supper or dinner later, so the bread and butter was cut thinly, and not so much was eaten. In later Victorian times when people were not so strict about travelling, Sunday tea-time became a good time to go visiting friends and relatives.

Tea in the garden.

SERVANTS

Servants with the daughter of the house, 1898.

Everybody who could afford to would employ servants to work for them. Sometimes a household would have just one servant, but in large houses there could be dozens. With many servants to do the work, Victorian meals were elaborate and often took hours to prepare. Sometimes the servants were given less work on Sunday. If the main meal was at 1.30 pm instead of in the evening, there could be a cold supper, leaving the servants free all afternoon.

CHURCH
AND CHAPEL

Religion played a part in almost every Victorian child's life. Most families would go to church or chapel at least once on a Sunday. Children were expected to behave like adults in church. Imagine sitting on a hard seat for over an hour without fidgeting or whispering once.

Church at Brading, Isle of Wight.

ATTENDING CHURCH OR CHAPEL

Most Christians in England and Wales belonged to the Church of England and went to their parish church. Others chose the new chapels with their lively preaching and simpler services. There were also Catholics in most areas.

Not everybody went to church or chapel each week. One Sunday in 1851, everybody in the country who attended church or chapel was counted. Just over 40 people in every hundred went to a service on that day. If you lived in a town perhaps no one noticed if you missed church. In villages, children were sometimes punished at school on Monday for missing church on Sunday.

INSIDE A CHURCH

In the Church of England the best pews were bought or rented. Wealthy people made themselves comfortable in pews with cushions. Poor people often felt less welcome. Those who could not afford to pay for seats stayed at the back, sometimes standing. Some people turned to the new Methodist or Baptist chapels because they felt that God was more interested in whether they were good than whether they were rich.

The interior of a church.

A church in the Scottish highlands.

THE CHURCH IN SCOTLAND

In Scotland, the Episcopal Church had very similar services to those of the Church of England. But the Episcopal Church was not the main Church of Scotland. The Church of Scotland was, and still is, Presbyterian. Not everybody attended these churches – some attended the Roman Catholic Church, while others attended the new chapels or the Free Church which was started up in 1843.

Children singing in church.

THE CHURCH SERVICE

Hymns were sung in church but, between the hymns, services in England followed the Prayer Book closely. In the Presbyterian Church in Scotland, they did not follow liturgy or the Prayer Book.

Nonconformist chapel services had more variety, with visiting preachers. Sometimes people told the story of how they changed from a sinful life and started to believe in Jesus. Sermons were preached in both church and chapel. The preachers tried to stir up people's feelings, making them ashamed of wrongdoing, grateful for God's gifts, or afraid of Hell if they died as sinners.

CITY MISSIONS

Both the Church of England and the Nonconformist churches were worried that there were more and more people in Britain who did not believe in God or know about Jesus. Perhaps they saw children in crowded parts of big cities whose parents never attended church, were often drunk and unable to teach their children right from wrong. City Missions were set up and preachers went to the poorest areas to persuade people to come to special services.

Poster for a City Mission meeting.

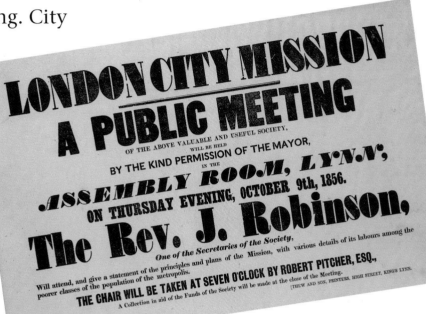

The first page from the catechism.

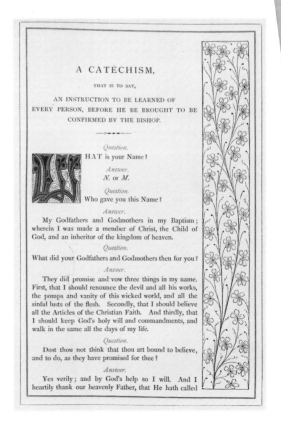

THE CATECHISM

Children were expected to learn to understand what it meant to be a Christian. To help them they were taught the catechism, which you can find in the Book of Common Prayer. It is a set of questions and answers to be learned by heart. As well as helping their children to learn the catechism, some parents made them learn parts of the Bible or prayers from the week's service.

SUNDAY
SCHOOL

Would you like to go to school on Sunday? For some Victorian children this was their only chance to learn to read and write. It was also a chance to mix with other children on a day when most games were forbidden. If you went every week you might get a prize, and there was also the Sunday School treat to look forward to.

TEACHING IN THE SUNDAY SCHOOL

Children were sent to Sunday School even if their parents did not usually go to church. In the early part of Victoria's reign there were few non-fee paying schools for children. The churches and chapels found that to teach children to read the Bible they first had to teach them to read. The younger children would take slates to write on. Parents found it useful to send their children out, giving them an hour's peace at home. There were morning and afternoon Sunday Schools, so if children went to church in the morning, they would go to Sunday School in the afternoon.

Children off to Sunday School.

SUNDAY SCHOOL LESSONS

The Sunday School teacher, in 1885.

In church Sunday Schools the job of teacher was often taken on by the clergyman's wife or daughter. Teachers at chapel Sunday Schools were chosen because they were true Christians, but they were often poorly educated. Bright pupils sometimes knew more than their teachers. All that most teachers had to help them were copies of the Bible or the catechism. The children were divided into groups of the same age. Some groups were led by older pupils, called monitors, or by assistant teachers.

SUNDAY SCHOOL REWARDS

Children who had been to school all week might have preferred not to go to Sunday School. To encourage them to go, Sunday Schools gave prizes for attendance and good behaviour. The best children would be given certificates like this one and, often, a book as a reward. There would also be a treat or an outing once a year.

Just as in ordinary schools at that time, the teacher would keep a cane handy to punish children who did not pay attention or were cheeky.

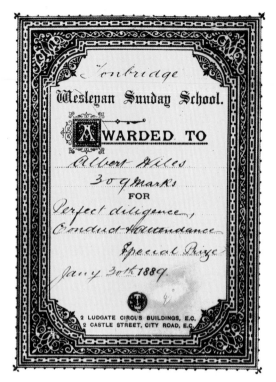

An attendance certificate.

HYMN SINGING

Singing hymns made a change from Bible study. Many hymns for children were written at this time. For example:

Do no sinful action,
Speak no angry word;
Ye belong to Jesus,
Children of the Lord.

Christ is kind and gentle,
Christ is pure and true,
And His little children
Must be holy too.

Singing in Sunday School in 1896.

SUNDAY MAGAZINES

Magazines like this one were written to encourage children to care about people less fortunate than themselves. In the magazine, they would read about children in slums who were not taught about Jesus. There were also stories about children whose parents were unable to care for them because of drinking alcohol. Some Victorian Christians encouraged children to make a solemn promise that they would never drink alcohol.

From 1847 they called the organization against alcohol the 'Band of Hope'. It started in Leeds, and gradually gained branches all over the country.

Our Own Magazine,
1894.

TREATS AND OUTINGS

How many times do you go on an outing each year? Victorian treats may sound tame compared with the theme parks and fairgrounds of today, but Victorian children enjoyed these special occasions. Once a year, every Sunday School celebrated the day it was founded. Every church and chapel also had a Sunday School treat. Lucky children were taken on a trip as well as being given an especially good tea.

THE PARADE

This Sunday School is celebrating the day it was founded. The day began with a parade of handsome banners. The children would stop and sing carefully-practised hymns. Some children might recite poems, on their own or in pairs, before tea. Children who had recited were sometimes rewarded with an orange.

Celebrating the founding of a Sunday School in 1871.

SUNDAY SCHOOL TREAT

Part of the excitement of the Sunday School treat was getting to it. In country areas farm horses and wagons were often used. When several Sunday Schools joined together there would be a long and merry procession of wagons laden with children on benches. Children from one Hampshire village used to be taken to the seaside behind a steam traction engine. Unfortunately the sparks burnt holes in their clothes!

A steam traction engine.

CANAL BOAT TRIP

These children from a church Sunday School were taken on a canal boat. When tea was unpacked, the children had more bread, butter and cake than most of them were used to.

Children on a canal boat.

After tea there were games. Perhaps there would be 'scrambling' after sweets and nuts thrown by a teacher. Then the children might stand in a circle for traditional round games like Jenny-sits-a-weeping, or play chasing games like tag.

SUNDAY PASTIMES

For Victorians, Sunday was a holiday from school and work but it was also a holy day. Children were brought up to be quiet and serious on Sunday. Most of their usual pastimes were forbidden. There were few toys or games, almost no books, no sports, travel or entertainment. This meant there was very little to do once you had been to church and Sunday School. So how did Victorian families pass the long slow hours of Sunday?

SATURDAY EVENING

Here is a working man's family on Saturday night. Before bedtime, the boys' bricks, the little girl's doll and mother's mending will all be put away until Monday. The next evening, Sunday, they will gather round the fire again. The big Bible will be down from the shelf and perhaps another book kept specially for Sunday. The children amuse themselves looking at the pictures.

A working class family at home, 1861.

On Sunday the children will talk quietly so as not to disturb father reading his Sunday newspaper. Perhaps before bedtime father puts aside his paper and reads aloud from the Bible. Then the children go to bed and say their prayers, pleased that the long day is over.

SUNDAY TOYS

Luckily, there were some toys which were allowed because they taught children stories from the Bible. A Noah's Ark, with Noah, his family and all the pairs of animals, as shown to the right, was a favourite. There were also jigsaws and brick puzzles which fitted together to show scenes from the life of Jesus. This one shows Jesus raising a child from the dead.

Noah's Ark

Building blocks with a religious picture.

AFTERNOON WALK

In the afternoon many families went for a walk. These Londoners are taking their walk in Hyde Park. The boys are being allowed to sail model yachts. Perhaps some of the passers-by think it is an unsuitable thing to do on Sunday. But even if you had to walk along on your best behaviour it was better than staying indoors with next to nothing to do. You could see your friends and neighbours and show off your best clothes. What Victorian children dreaded above all was a *wet* Sunday.

A walk in the park.

A family picnic.

A PICNIC

One of the things a family could do together on Sunday was have a picnic. They would pack buns and sandwiches into a basket and walk to a favourite place. People tried not to travel by carriage or train on Sunday unless the journey was very important. But most Victorians lived quite close to their relations, and it was easy to meet them for a picnic tea.

Some families were stricter than others and looked on disapprovingly while others enjoyed themselves. As Victoria's reign went on, people became a little less strict about Sunday. Then it became more usual to go visiting and invite people for meals on Sundays.

READING BOOKS

Children were encouraged to read books which taught them about their religion. *The Pilgrim's Progress* was found in many homes, but it was written by John Bunyan in the seventeenth century and is difficult to read. The hero is called Christian and his adventures show what it is like trying to be a Christian. There were books written specially for children to read on Sundays. Mrs Sherwood copied John Bunyan and wrote *The Infant's Progress*. She also wrote *The Fairchild Family*, a very popular set of stories to show how three children learned to be good.

The first page from *The Pilgrim's Progress*.

MUSIC

Many better-off families enjoyed music. There were no radios or recordings in Victorian times, so the family had to make its own music. Only religious music was allowed on Sundays. The family would gather round the piano, taking turns to choose favourite hymns to sing.

Family music.

GOOD-NIGHT PRAYERS

Victorian parents made sure their children said their prayers before they went to sleep. Every night a child would say the Lord's Prayer, beginning 'Our Father', and would ask God to bless all the family. Another prayer often used by children at this time was:

Good-night prayers.

Gentle Jesus meek and mild,
Look upon this little child.
Pity my simplicity;
Suffer me to come to thee.

Many children learnt this by heart without understanding it. A simpler bedtime prayer was:

Now I lay me down to
    sleep,
I pray the Lord my soul to
    keep;
And if I die before I wake,
I pray the Lord my soul to
    take.

TIME LINE

EARLY 1800s

1803 Sunday School Union formed to help Sunday Schools in London and elsewhere and to provide books.

1818 Mrs Sherwood's *The Fairchild Family* published (Part One).

1819 Queen Victoria born.

1829 Catholic Emancipation Act passed, which let Catholics become Members of Parliament.

1830s

1831 Lord's Day Observance Society founded to help keep Sunday a day for rest and worship.

1833 Oxford Movement in Church of England begins. Its aim was to restore the Catholic tradition and ritual of the Church.

1837 Queen Victoria's reign begins.

1840s

1846 Evangelical Alliance formed. This was an international group to support Christians who thought that belief in the Bible was more important than ritual.

The boys' sailor suit was made popular by the young Prince of Wales.

1847 The 'Band of Hope' started.

1850s

1851 A census shows 40 per cent of people in Britain attend church or chapel.

Queen Victoria's purchase of Balmoral in Scotland makes wearing tartan fashionable.

1854 Holman Hunt painted *The Light of the World,* a picture of Jesus which became very popular.

1000				1500						2000
1066					1485	1603	1714	1837	1901	

NORMANS — MIDDLE AGES — TUDORS — STUARTS — GEORGIANS — VICTORIANS — 20TH CENTURY

1860s

1859-65 Mrs Beeton's Cookery Book published and printed three times.

1861 Dr Barnardo's East End Mission to help homeless boys in London.

1866 *Alice in Wonderland* by Lewis Carroll published.

1870s

1871 Bank Holidays introduced.

1874 Public Worship Regulation Act to make sure that clergymen of the Church of England did not bring Catholic customs into their services.

1878 William Booth founds the Salvation Army.

1880s

1883 Foundation of the Boy's Brigade.

1886 *Little Lord Fauntleroy* published, making velvet suits popular for boys.

1890s

1896 Museums and art galleries allowed to open on Sundays.

1900s

1901 Queen Victoria dies.

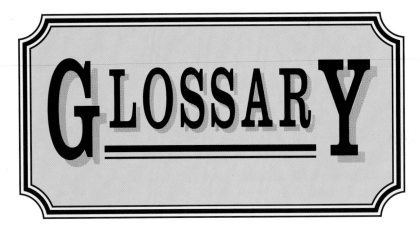

GLOSSARY

Attendance Being present at an event.

Catholic Christians who follow the leadership of the Pope.

Clergyman A man whose job it is to hold services in the Church of England and to look after the people of the parish.

Combinations Underwear made up of vest and pants together, often made of cotton or woollen material.

Duty A task, or way of behaving suitable to who you are.

Episcopal A Church governed by bishops.

Fowls Chickens.

Garnished Decorated.

Lard Pig's fat. Cottage housewives would make a year's supply when they killed their pig.

Liturgy The form of service laid down by the church.

Missions Groups of Christians working to persuade others to become Christian.

Muffins Plain buns made with yeast.

Nonconformists Methodists, Baptists and other Christians who broke away from the Church of England.

Parish Division of the country which has its own church.

Protestant The Christians who, since the sixteenth century, refused to accept the leadership of the Pope.

Presbyterian Protestant Church with lay elders (senior members who are not clergymen).

Range A coal-burning stove, often with several ovens and a water boiler.

Recite To say out loud something which has been learned by heart.

Slates Thin pieces of stone slate, usually mounted in a frame, used by schoolchildren to write on.

Slums Overcrowded houses, often without drains or water supply.

Stays A firm padded vest, laced up the front, worn by girls.

BOOKS TO READ

Chamberlin, E. *Everyday Life in the Nineteenth Century* (Macdonald Educational, 1983)

Conner, E. A. *A Child in Victorian London* (Wayland, 1986)

Evans, D. *How We Used To Live – Victorians Early and Late* (A & C Black, 1989)

Harper, R. *Finding Out About Victorian Childhood* (Batsford, 1986)

Ross, S. *Spotlight on the Victorians* (Wayland, 1988)

Thompson, F. To Church on Sunday (Chapter XIV) in *Lark Rise to Candleford* (1939); also Chapter XXI, Over To Candleford

Triggs, T. *Victorian Britain* (Wayland, 1990)

PLACES TO VISIT

The following museums have displays and exhibitions to do with social history.

ENGLAND

Avon: Blaise Castle House, Henby, Bristol, BS10 7QS. Tel. 0272 506789

Cheshire: Quarry Bank Mill, Styal, SK9 4LA. Tel. 0625 527468

County Durham: North of England Open Air Museum, Beamish, DH9 ORG. Tel. 0207 231811

Humberside: Wilberforce House, 25 High Street, Hull, HU1 3EP. Tel: 0482 593902

Lancashire: Museum of Childhood, Lancaster, LA1 1YS. Tel. 0524 32808

London: Victoria and Albert Museum, South Kensington, SW7 2RL. Tel. 071 938 8500

Museum of Childhood, Cambridge Heath Road, London E2 9PA. Tel. 081 980 2415

Merseyside: Toy Museum, 42 Bridge Street Row, Chester, CH1 1RS. Tel. 0244 346297

Norfolk: Gressenhall Rural Life Museum, Dereham, NR20 4DR. Tel. 0362 860563

Shropshire: Iron Bridge Gorge Museum, Blists Hill Site, Telford, TS8 7AW. Tel. 0952 433522

Warwickshire: St. John's House Museum, Warwick, CV34 4NF. Tel. 0926 412034

Yorkshire: York Castle Museum, York, YO1 1RY. Tel: 0904 653611

SCOTLAND

Angus: Angus Folk Museum, Glamis, Forfar, DD8 1RT. Tel. 037 84288

WALES

Cardiff: Welsh Folk Museum, St. Fagans, CF5 6XB. Tel. 0222 569441

INDEX